Employee to Entrepreneur

Rohit Mehta

Employee to Entrepreneur

(How to supercharge your life and become a successful entrepreneur)

Author: Rohit Mehta

Website: www.bloggermehta.com

Published By: Self – Published
Address: Pirhi, Patna, Bihar -801102

First Edition: 2021

Price: ₹ 190/ -

ISBN: **978-93-5578-174-1**

Printer: Sunil Block works & Printers, Patna-6

Contents

Say Goodbye to Your 9 to 5 Jobs

If you're tired of your regular job and are looking for a way to escape and leave the life of your dreams, then you're reading the right book. You don't have to be stuck in the office all day hating your job I'm thinking that there's no way out, there definitely is! And you are your own escape plan, that's right.

If you really want to live the life that you envision and make real substantial income, then your 9 to 5 is not the answer. Nowadays there are so many ways that you can move from you 9 to 5 into starting your own business that can thrive depending on how much effort and time you put in. Now more and more people are becoming financially free and living life on their own terms without having to lose quality time in life or miss out on making memorable moments.

Life is way too short to be worrying about you your future and how you going to live in regards to money. Today is the day to get clued up on investment and entrepreneurship and take your life in a different direction regardless of what you've been told. It doesn't matter how old you are or where you live in, the only thing stopping you, is you!

So what are you waiting for? If you really want to transform your life and grow your wealth then you have to do something extraordinary, meaning you have to come out of your comfort zone and do something different then what you're used to. You can't change your life by sitting in those doing nothing and waiting for wolf to mysteriously appear, you have to be proactive and put in 100% into what you do in order to reap successful results.

Shifting your Mindset

The idea of setting up a business might sound amazing, it might sound fun and exciting. Many people want to become financially independent, and for good reasons too including having more time. You might be thinking to yourself "Is this something that you really want to embark on?", or "Is this something that you am capable of making work?"There are differences when it comes to the mindsets of employees and entrepreneur. Is it your dream to start a business? or is there an element of doubt lingering in your mind?

You're excited to talk about your ideas but there's something stopping you from moving forward. It might be your desire be an entrepreneur but realise that this is something that if you went born into an entrepreneurial household, it may not be second nature to you. You have to learn about what it takes to become a successful entrepreneur. You're mind can become restless especially when you don't know where or how to start.

You might not have a good support network to give you that extra push. Your gut instinct doesn't lie, you know that the normal job path that you should be taking but something just doesn't sit right. You don't really know what it is you and this is where a support network could have been a useful tool to motivate you. You know that entrepreneurship is for you but don't know how to achieve your goal.

This is where your thinking comes in. You're thinking that you should be an entrepreneur, you see a lot of people like yourself talking about how they want to become financially independent and start a business. Maybe you are attempting this and you're starting on this venture and it just feels so uncomfortable. The more you dig into what it takes to become successful the scary of things become to you. you find out that there's a lot to being a business owner and entrepreneur then you thought.

Yes, entrepreneurship is amazing and a great choice, however, don't get me wrong, it's very hard. As an employee you can contribute greatly to Society, of course, but you also have other skills that are useful too. All these skills can contribute so much to people's lives and is a gap that's not being filled. You have the opportunity to change people's lives if you want to. Some people need to be told what to do, some people really do rely on someone telling them "You need you to study this" or "This is how you need to do that" and so on.

Such people like to be given instructions on how to operate in the world so many people can agree with this. If you don't like being told what to do you might struggle when somebody tries to give you orders or instructions. That rebellious part of you comes out and you start resisting. They're always science of somebody being made to be an entrepreneur and one of these is they usually don't like being ruled over by a boss. You might be working long hour days almost every day, for about a decade, but your body is begging for a change.

Full control of your time is essential and many people say that a 9-5 is robbing them of their time. When you're an entrepreneur you have full control of your time, it is up to you to decide when you want to work, how much you work and the efficiency of your hard work. You can take breaks whenever you want, you can have holidays or vacations whenever you please as long as it works around your schedule. Now, as an employee you realise that being a workaholic actually kind of sucks and you have the device a plan to escape pat nine to five lifestyle and really start living your life.

In business you have to figure out what you are capable of and how you can put boundaries in place, put the right operations in place so you don't have to be there every second of everyday to run your business. When it comes to making money, there is no ceiling as to how much money can be made as an entrepreneur, there is very much a ceiling when it comes to being an employee. If you're not making anything move in your life or improving your marketing and sales ability, then things won't happen. You've got to make things happen and be the change.

Create a really valuable product that meets people's needs and you could be making the big bucks from that, really large amounts of money. You learn so much about business though it might be a steep learning curve at first. Whatever you know how to do, use this talent to make money. You might be a great graphic designer, you might also be the only person in your company to start with. You are all of it until you get to a certain point where you can start delegating but even then, you might have to step in at anytime and fulfil a role that isn't being completed properly because maybe a staff member might get sick.

You have to be able to do everything, and because of that, the amount of knowledge you acquire will be vast and you'll come to love learning. Some of the best entrepreneurs in the world got to where they are today because of the knowledge that they sought, and they utilised in their life. Business can sometimes be stressful but you get that thrill too and hang onto the edge of your sea. You know that it's also stressful but you're doing something you love so it's worth it. As employees you might be thing that you'll hopefully love your job one day but you don't come across many employees that are jumping with excitement to go to work so that's kind of lucky.

Being able to remain yourself in business is one of the best feelings ever. This is what freedom is and freedom is the number one thing that you desire in life and business gives you the capacity to do that. You will not change yourself in order to fulfil customers' needs because that is the freedom that you have as entrepreneur. You get to still be yourself while providing value from for you and people around you. If you're still like "Yeah that sounds awesome but I'm not sure if I can make the shift" then you need to shift your mindset from employee to entrepreneur.

The difference in the mindset of an entrepreneur's mindset from an employee is that as an entrepreneur you do just what you say and you're not afraid to take risks. If you've never been an employee, you just can't speak about it the same way somebody that has lived that 9-5 life can because you lack experience as an employee. If you've spent a good portion of your life working for somebody else It's never too late to develop an entrepreneurial mindset. The security versus freedom mindset is a constant struggle for some. However, if your number one driver in life is freedom, you want to have freedom on every aspect, whether it's freedom of your mind or freedom of movement.

Whether it's freedom from any entities or freedom from authority, you desperately want freedom in every way. It's not to say that you don't want security as an entrepreneur, of course you have bills to pay. You want to have security in short and long run, and you want to be responsible fully and wholeheartedly for your retirement. You don't want to be 100 years old and struggling, you should have passed the working phased of your life by then. With enough motivation, knowledge and persistence, you should have yourself set up perfectly well for retirement. In this way, you'll be able to sit down and relax and enjoy your old age.

Love freedom and you aspire to have freedom. Most people have not been brought up with this concept, the majority of the world is stuck on one path in life and they don't really question it because they might not have anyone around to provide them with extra information on how things could be done. The usually go to school, then a great university, get a good job, climb the corporate ladder and rely on the government to pay them during their pension. Then the cycle continues and they pass on the same mindset to their kids.

An entrepreneurial mindset

What does it mean to be an entrepreneur? It is not for the faint in hearted, it is only for the brave, the courageous, the calculated, it is reserved for the resilient. There are two sides to the coin of entrepreneurship, there's heads and there's tails but most people fail to see tails. Those that see heads, they live on the surface, the lights, the cameras, the action, the yachts and the fame but they don't want to sweat to get what they want. Anybody that is willing to make the sacrifices, they stay up late, they work longer and are more focused. They pay the price and get the job done and finish what they started, those are the ones who succeed.

if you're going to be an entrepreneur, you're going to need to lead, the world needs more creative, resilient, and passionate leaders. We need committed, focused, and disruptive entrepreneurs. The last thing we need is somebody to come along with another good idea but they don't have the passion and perseverance to get the job done. If you don't have passion, then you don't want to be a disruptive entrepreneur and you want to step into a room with a new idea and challenge the status quo but you don't have passion.

Right now, you may be in pain, right now you may be hurting but if you have vision, you are able to see past the pain and look into the eyes of the future. Your perspective can either become your prison or your passport, it can either arrest you or release you. Possibility is destiny and it is fear that keeps us arrested and apprehended by the spirit of impossibility. You will inherit the future if you know where you want to be financially, if you know where you want to be emotionally, if you know where you want to be physically, relationally socially, 10 times out of 10 it is because you have settled in a place called convenience.

If you're at this stage, you've gotten lazy and sometimes praise can be poison. It keeps you locked in a state of paralysis and you shine in trophies from the past and that's why you always hear those people from the past say things like, "I remember back in the day when I used to do this" still shining the trophy of the past accomplishments so sometimes we can receive praise like a venomous snake that injects its poisonous venom in our veins and in our heart and causes us to stay locked in a state of paralysis when it comes to progress.

This is what happens when people keep telling you things like "Oh, You did so well ten years ago," If you continue to believe that your best work is behind you, then you never achieve what is ahead of you. You have to get crystal clear about your future because the only reason why you are alive is because you have work to do and you have to figure out why on earth you are here. What is your destiny? You've got have a shark mentality because if a shark swims backwards, it dies. A shark can only move forward and so I need you every single day you wake up go after what you want in life.

When you are hungry, you are innovative. When you are hungry, when you are no longer full, when you are no longer satisfied with where you are and you raise your standards, and this makes your future bright. If you want a future, then you are going to have to get acquainted with pain, discomfort and inconvenience because hunger is the only thing that's going to give you the power to persevere through that pain and never stop climbing the hill of success. There will always another hill the climb to find so you have to be hungry for your dream, you have to be eager to get to the next level in whatever you want to achieve. Don't always be on the lookout for failure, every day you should be hungry to learn, you have to be hungry to read and you have to be hungry to learn. You have to be hungry to manifest what is in your mind including all your goals and aspirations. read a manifest what is in your head. When you're full you can't receive, when you're full you lose vision when your full, you get lazy when you're full and you procrastinate when you're full. This is the kind of mindset you need to have as an entrepreneur, and you will forever thrive in whatever you put your mind on. If you can think it, you can achieve it, then do it!

Which Mindset Do You Have?

The mentalities of an employee or an entrepreneur are in some cases very different and also the motivations are also different. Now, the conditions for success can also be different so one is not particularly better than the other, all the same, let's explore some of these differences. With employees it depends a lot on the size of the company, if you work for big multinational corporation some of these things will be even pushed to the extreme, smaller start-ups maybe not so much. As the individual, you as the employee are really part of a larger team or in some cases part of a large corporation. If you're an entrepreneur, in many cases you are the team or a very significant part of the team. For an employee the goals of the business are really set by the direction of the financial markets, for example, Wall Street are set by the board of directors but as an entrepreneur the goals are really set by you.

You have to come up with a strategy for growth, a strategy for development and follow through with those goals. Your actions as an employee are really directed by your manager, they're directed by other people in your organisations or in your division but as an entrepreneur — though your activities your actions are really self-directed and self-prioritised— you are not being told what to do by anybody. as an employee your role itself is one of its specialist so usually as part of a larger team your role and what you do is generally more specialised but as an entrepreneur you will find yourself wearing a whole lot of different hats, you tend to be more of a generalist and less specialised. you may have to do sales and account management financing, design, product development or manufacturing or whatever it is that goes around your particular business.

You're going to be wearing a lot of hats and you have to learn a lot of different roles. Now, in terms of support, as an employee there may be many departments in many supportive elements within that organisation from HR to production to sales to merchandising too. There can be a lot of support for you as an employee but as an entrepreneur there is less you really have to go out and find your support you have to find your specialists. You have to find people to teach you whatever it is that you don't know how to do or you have to be able to somehow locate and develop relationships with people who do know how to do those things.

Now, in terms of impact, the kind of impact that you can have as an employee or an entrepreneur if you're an employee the impact that you have is really mitigated by the number of people in your company so your impact is generally smaller, it's lower as part of a whole but as an entrepreneur you have a great deal of ownership and say your impact on the business is significant. The complexity of being an entrepreneur versus the complexity of being employee is also quite different as an employee that complexity of what you do or the environment that you're working in is pretty complex, meaning some corporations can be a very complicated matrix to navigate.

Sometimes lots of different even international locations and departments that are in are working with each other and navigating that environment can be complex and take a lot of learning. As an entrepreneur that structural organisation is very much simplified and also may totally reside within you so navigating that is really more about juggling the hats that you're wearing in terms of what you're doing now. when it comes to personal growth as an employee your personal growth is really more linear; it's based on the usual corporate ladder, moving up from position to position within a specialised range but as an entrepreneur your path of growth is really usually less linear and it's more learning based and more based on the success of your business and the growth of your business.

One of the key things about the differences between entrepreneurs and employees is risk when you are an employee. The company is really bearing most of the risk and you have lower exposure to any kind of financial up turn downturn or any kind of change in the environment or any kind of impact on that companies business, you have less risk. As an entrepreneur you have a great deal of exposure and a much higher risk in terms of what happens in terms of your business, business environment and revenue. When it comes to compensation, the differences between an employee and entrepreneur are pretty significant to compensation when your employee is predictable. It's based on the health of your company and the level of your role but you're going to get a paycheque every couple weeks and it's going to have benefits and it's going to be predictable. You don't always know what you're going to get as an entrepreneur, it may be determined by the fluctuations in revenue in your business or the number of clients you can bring in and bold projects that you can work the number of products that you have.

The success of those products is unpredictable and so it can really fluctuate, there's much more risk involved in terms of compensation. Employees and entrepreneurs, when it comes to the hours they put into, are quite different. It's not being implied here that as an employee you never work long hours because you absolutely do, you can have very long hours but the hours are really more mapped out even though you may have to put in more their regular set as an employee. As an entrepreneur they are irregular and they are they fluctuate a lot and you may have to put in a lot of extra time because you are wearing all those hats and because everything is relying on you. when it comes down to it, the core skills sets of an entrepreneur our ambition, self-motivation and being strategic, so being able to develop, achieve and motivate yourself to go for your own goals and being really resourceful are very much needed.

Finding the help of the specialist that you need there outside of the range of what you can do as an individual is the reality of being an entrepreneur. You're more of a generalist, right? You wear more hats your self-directed more in your learning, so you have to understand what you need to learn what you don't know and go about in finding that knowledge. Your tolerance for risk has to be a lot higher. Now, this core skill sets of an employee or a little bit different you have to be open to being a team player you have to be willing to take direction you have to pursue with energy and vigour. goals that are set by other people, you generally tend to be more of a specialist, so you have to know a lot about a more finite range of things. You also have to be politically adept so like I said you've got to be able to navigate sometimes through a matrix than complicated political and organisational systems and environments. You have to many times adopt the company culture, whatever that company culture is sometimes they call it "Drinking the Kool-Aid".

You have to personify the culture of the company that you work for rather than like an entrepreneur setting that company culture, then you also have to really have to thrive in a structured environment. Which one of these roles is best for you, being an employee or being an entrepreneur? Ask yourself questions such as:

- How much does it take to get you out of bed in the morning and to get doing what you're supposed to be doing?
- Do you have a broad range of knowledge?
- Do you know a little bit about marketing, finance, sales and product service?
- Do you have the motivation to learn those things?

How to Quit your 9 to 5?

You want be an investor or maybe entrepreneur and you want to build your wealth and you want to be financially free and all that good stuff, the only problem is you're stuck at a job right now and you need the paycheque and you can't stand your job. What do you do? and how do you quit? Well, if you want to quit your job, the first thing you have to do is to figure out why you were at your job. For most of you, it's because you need a paycheque. If you weren't working, you wouldn't be getting paid and you wouldn't have money to eat. That could be a problem, so for most of you you're at a job because you need a paycheque, while for others you might be at your jobs because you invested a lot of time and have a lot of money saved up or invested.

Maybe all of your friends are working jobs so if you weren't working you just be sitting at home watching TV all day and that just makes you feel miserable so you don't know what you would be doing if you didn't have a job. For some of you, you might be at a job to learn, maybe you love what you do or you're trying to learn a new skill and if this is you, you're probably not worried about how you're going to quit your job. If you are keep watching if you're working a job because you need money, the first thing you have to do is to figure out how much money you actually need.

There are two numbers you need to look at. The first is what you call your ideal number, this is how much money you're making at your job right now that if you were making the same amount of money outside of your job well then you can do other things wearing your lifestyle or standard of living. Let's say you make $5000 from your job so this is your ideal number, this isn't the cap to how much you want to make but it gives you a good ideal kind of starting point for how much you should be aiming to make. The second number you have to figure out is your minimum number, what is the minimum amount of money you need to survive today? If you were fired from your job tomorrow and you had to cut back on your expenses and had to find a find a way to make ends meet how much money do you need to keep things going.

Let's say this number is $1500, that is a survival number. Now that you have your ideal number and your survival number, you know that you need to be making somewhere between $1500 and $5000 outside of your job to be able to quit your job, that's fine but the question is, "How well can you invest your money?" Let's say you got a reasonable 7% annual return on your money meaning if you invested $1 you get $1.07 back then you would need to invest around $255,000 to get your survival number of $1500 a month and you'd have to invest close to $850,000 to get your ideal number of $5000 a month. This is your standard attire but model where you work to save or invest enough money until you have enough income or interest or profit coming back into your pocket to survive.

It's cool and it works but you don't want you to wait 30 years to be able to live your life so if you want to quit your job and start living your life, investing and smart financial planning is very important but it will only get you halfway there. If you want to start living your life sooner rather than later, then you're going to have to create more income from something that you enjoy doing. Imagine that you are a big fan of cooking but you hate your customer service job, well one thing that you can do as you can start a cooking business on the side. You can do this during weekends, evenings and during your free time. Yes, it is hard and it will take time but it is possible and then when you get your profit to $1500 a month consistently now you're ready to quit your job.

You can then invest extra time that you have because now you don't have to go to work. You can grow the incomparable cooking business to at least your ideal number of $5000 this way you can maintain your same lifestyle, let me show you what this means with some numbers if you sell a cooking book or a cooking pan or special German chocolate cake and you only make $25 of profit per product sold, well, you will have to sell two products a day to make enough money to survive so you can quit your job if you can make $50 per profit per product sold. Then you'll only have to sell one product today to make enough money to survive and if you can make $100 per product sold, then you only have to make one sale every two days to make enough money to hit your survival number so you can quit your job and then grow your business full time now.

This is much easier said than done but it is very possible for you. These numbers are very reasonable but you have to stay consistent and keep putting in that time when you have free time like evenings, weekends and holidays to make it happen like if Amazon can sell 6000 products a minute on a good day which is about 9 million products a day then you can keep working towards your goal. Here's another thing that you want you to understand, going from zero to 1 sale a day is going to be 10 times harder than growing from one sale a day to 10 sales a day because getting off the ground and getting started is the hardest part and if you're not ready to create your cooking product yet, you're still not out of luck, you can sell it.

The cooking service industry is the easiest to get into but

it's not the easiest to do forever. It is the easiest to start because now you're going to take your own talents and the things that you know you're going to start monetising on them. Now, you can cater for your friends parties or you can make meals for people in your area. This is a way that you can get started without having to invest a whole bunch of money or time figuring out how to create a product. Once you know what you want to do there's just one last step that you have to take if you want to get to the point that you can quit your job. You have to take action. You have to get to work even if it's exhausting at the beginning and you're tired, you have to keep on pushing.

It's like being at college during the day and working on a business during the evenings; it takes time and commitment. It's exhausting but if you really want to get to the point where you can quit your job you have to be the one to stop bingeing Netflix after work and start bingeing business books and business courses and invest time into growing your business. If you can do that and you stay consistent and you keep growing one small baby step at a time. This is just the numbers game until you get to the point where you're ready quit your job and that opportunities really become limitless because now you're not getting paid by the amount of hours you work, you're getting paid by the amount of value created and there's no limit to what you can do.

One of my biggest challenges people face is filtering through the get rich quick schemes and everybody and their parents talking about making money online or getting rich with real estate. For some reason, 99% of businesses advise people on how easy it is to make, it's all about how to get rich fast with minimal effort. All these so called gurus trick you into thinking that it's easy. Well, here's a little spoiler alert, if it was that easy everybody would be doing it. It's not easy to get rich or start a business but thankfully there is a reliable way to escape your day job. There are steps you can take in your business that allows you to quit your job in as little as six months from now and do it without risking your savings or overworking yourself.

If you ever want to give your old job the sack the first thing you need to know is how to avoid success killing mistakes and traps okay. Success in business isn't necessarily about being smart, it's about not being a sucker and one of the biggest sucker moves is to start a business where the odds are stacked against you and everybody else trying to start that same type of business. What about successful businesses? There characterised by any business or event where only a small percentage of the people enjoy the majority of the rewards like in the book publishing industry where a few dozen authors sell millions of books while 98% of authors only sell a few 100 copies if any at all or an evolution where one species wins the genetic lottery and the rest of vanished forever.

Historians believe that we actually coexisted with Neanderthals until we humans decided we didn't want to share a planet anymore. Now there are billions of us and none of them. That's a winner take, all situation or in the tech industry where you have a few companies that dominate the market take a look at Amazon, for example, it's long been by far the largest bookstore on earth, now it's just running all kinds of industries and accounts for nearly half of all E-commerce growth. Amazon is a giant among ants and while it does have some competitors, there are few and far between the same phenomenon applies to anything where a small advantage leads to disproportionate results. No matter how skilled you are, or how prepared you are, or how hard you work, there is a tremendous amount of luck involved when the game goes in your favour.

Jeff Bezos is a great example, sure he's a smart dude but there are plenty of others just as smart and creative, they just didn't win the business lottery. Winners like Jeff get to live in mansions while thousands of losers get to go get a job. So, you want to start a tech company you want to create the next big app or maybe get a patent on some great idea that you have for an invention. If you want to guarantee your freedom in the next year, those are all terrible choices. Sure you may have recently heard of a story of another guy getting rich from the App Store but what about the other 10,000 people who barely made enough to buy a cup of coffee, you didn't hear about them because they're not writing blog posts or posting videos about how to get rich creating iPhone apps.

You never will hear from them unfortunately. It's hard to see things clearly when you only hear from the winners. This creates an illusion that everybody who works hard succeeds but it's not the case so if you want to escape your day job anytime soon, don't be a sucker and play a game you can actually have a chance of winning. Alright, let's talk about the second trap you're going to want to avoid, and that is passive income opportunities. There's no shortage of experts out there teaching how to make easy money, whether that's the real estate, YouTube drop shipping or selling niche products on Amazon. They're everywhere, this can all be amazing ways to create freedom in your life too.

The odds are actually pretty good if you actually stick it out long enough to reap the rewards but therein lies the problem you must stick it out for long enough. How long is long enough? Well, it's impossible to say but you should ask yourself are you willing to work your day job for at least three to five more years while spending all of your nights and weekends building a passive income business? If the answer is yes, that's great! If you're stuck in a job that you hate, you want the light at the end of the tunnel to at least be visible so you remember after you quit my job you started listening to podcasts and pretty soon you stumbled on the idea of starting an Internet business. The experts make it sound so easy like you could just put in some hard work for a few months and you could just coast out the rest of your life, cashing big cheques and working just a few hours per week.

Now you're thinking to yourself, life is going to be awesome. Why isn't everybody doing this? So, you start to work hard, really hard, you start learning about how to build a website. You write your first blog post and it doesn't take off and now you're upset. Luckily you didn't put all of your eggs in one basket and started another business at the same time because all that hard work didn't start paying off until four years after you got started. So for four years you basically worked for free and it's funny because every year you tell someone how great it's going to be when the work started paying off. Then the next year would come and success would still be just around the corner and sure there are people who do it faster but they are the exceptions.

The outliers, the ones who are in the right place, at the right time, and in the right niche with the right mentors. That's called luck, you cannot replicate look the truth is that it takes a lot of time effort dedication failure and learning to create passive income much more than you'll be led to believe and it's rarely ever completely passive. Anyway, is it worth? yes it is, you will love the business you build and the freedom it will give you, but if you're looking to quit your job anytime soon, there are much faster and easier paths. Unless you want to be stuck in your job for the next five years, you'll need something faster and with better odds of success.

What if you told you there was a low cost, low risk, fast and a nearly guaranteed way to build a business that frees you from your job. Within the next six months, there is a very simple concept here, start offering a service and charge money for it. That's it, it doesn't really matter what service either, as long as it pays well. You could build websites for small businesses, you can do wedding photography, you can do video editing, you can manage social media or even build excel spreadsheets. If that's what you're good at, then go for it!

You might love working with your hands and building and fixing stuff and it's a great business but there are thousands of services you can build a business from. Why is a service business the fastest easiest and most reliable way to escape your day job? Something is clear, when you try to invent some new service, you will have a low probability of success. If you opt for starting a common service, one where there are probably hundreds of competitors already and start offering that service, the fact that there are competitors means there is also demand. People have already demonstrated that they will pay for that service so when you start you start something like a handyman business, there can be dozens, if not hundreds of other handymen in your city.

Your business will flourish because you approach it in the right way. Now, you might think that if there is so much competition it would be harder to compete but here's a little secret about the service industry, most service providers suck. The good ones are busy all the time and the ones with availability are either just getting started or they're terrible to work with or they're simply not motivated to advertising growth. That leaves a lot of opportunity for the driven newcomer to succeed, you also don't need any crazy skills or credentials. In most cases you will need some skills you will need to be good at what you do and the service you're offering to your customers. You need a lot less skills than you think you do. Most skills can be learned pretty quickly in a matter of weeks, you remember them.

You don't have to be the best in the world just good enough to add value to your customers service businesses, also have really low risk. Offering a service is about as low risk as it gets, you don't need employees, you can work from your home, your office, or wherever it takes. It costs almost nothing to start and depending on the service you will probably need some tools or something, whether that is a computer or small hand tools, whatever service you have in mind you already have some of the tools necessary. Here's the best part, if it doesn't work and nobody hires you —which is pretty unlikely if you do it right— just try something else.

Another reason to start a service businesses is that the cash flow comes quickly. If you start an online business it may take you exactly three years to break $5000 in a single month and another two years before that happens consistently, so compared to other businesses you could start generating profit almost immediately to escape your job in as little as six months. Once you have your service business up and running and you've escaped your day job, you can use your new found free time to go after bigger ideas. Now, maybe you want to have a bigger impact in the world okay you don't need to run a service business for the rest of your life after being in business for over a year as a handyman. You start scheduling jobs more efficiently and you increase your rates and as a result you will be able to generate a full-time income.

Quitting your 9 to 5 job is just the first step in your entrepreneurial journey. There is much more that needs to be done to be successful call mom including successfully shifting your mindset from that of an employee to an entrepreneur. Inevitably the only thing that is stopping you from succeeding as an entrepreneur is yourself, you have the power to make the real difference. There are many people out there themselves "I wish I just started that business" or "Why didn't I just go to that networking event?" it is regret that keeps us from moving forward in life, dreams that should have been built yet have been wasted.

Map out your 9 to 5 escape plan and go off to your dreams wholeheartedly if there's anyone that can make a major difference in your life, it's you!

How to Become an Entrepreneur?

If you're creating a company or if you're joining a company, the most important thing is to attract great people. There are great people everywhere that's willing to excel in life, you just have to locate them. Create a new business and becoming a successful entrepreneur it's not a walk in a park, it requires time, enthusiasm, motivation and a creative mind.

We can look at some of the most successful entrepreneurs till date and as much as we admired them we can't ignore their journey and their struggle. Every entrepreneur has a story to tell at most will tell you how hard it was at the beginning but this improved with time Who's there journey that is not easy stop he from beginning to end, there are always hurdles and sometimes setbacks. If you want to be an entrepreneur, you have to think like an entrepreneur and act like an entrepreneur even if you don't see the resorts right away.

You have to be your greatest competition in the sense that you must challenge yourself every day to be a better person, to produce better results and to make things happen. Go after all the knowledge that you need to call never stop by leaving in yourself and your capability and set goals for yourself that are within your reach of achieving. It's when you think that you cannot achieve something that things just won't happen because she limit yourself, start seeing yourself as a winner and watch how things change around you, watch how things begin to manifest that you want.

Steps to Becoming an Entrepreneur

One of the best steps you can take is to be part of the entrepreneurship community and one of the ways that you can achieve personal freedom is by starting up your own business and what that allows you to do is set your own schedule, your end location, and put the people around you who you want to be around you. It gives you complete control over all aspects of your lives for so you're free to do anything. There are a lot of challenges with being an entrepreneur, while you may control your business aspect of things, you still report to your customers and your customers really are driving how you should act. When you start a business there are two options you can consider, one option is the traditional entrepreneur where you start a business and you own everything and then the other option is that you find an organisation that you work for and you work within entrepreneurial role.

You might know someone who worked for an agency in town and but now they've started up a new division there where they have created their own software and the beauty of that is they're getting a salary; they're getting regular income and still getting the experience of creating a business and creating an application without the same amount of risk as something like other entrepreneurs are doing. There are opportunities to be an entrepreneur while working for someone else so don't completely eliminate that option from your career especially you don't have steady income streams outside of your job to fall back on and if you have a family. There are organisations looking for people who are entrepreneurs who are looking to set up things and grow things so bear that in mind. What I would recommend.

If you want to get started you've got to put yourself around people who are entrepreneurial. You'll try to start up a business over the course of the weekend and it's a great way to meet other people who want to start a business. It's a great way to find out who works hard who actually does what they say they're going to do who are doers rather than talkers and helps you get ideas too. It's about getting you involved in the community. Align with people who are purpose driven and on the same wavelength as you, who are passionate about building a business so all these things give you opportunities to be around other like-minded people.

Entrepreneurship is hard, there are a lot of people who do it alone and find success, however, have a good team is a requirement to build a strong company because what's going to happen is you want to have these highs and these lows as you're building the company. You're going to need people to help you raise your lows. It's also a very lonely job being an entrepreneur when you're doing it alone, you're going to have stresses that you're not going to be able to open up in a lot of times you may not be in a position to talk it over with your spouse or your partner or loved one. They're really not going to understand the intricacies of building the business but from there that's going to be a starting point and then when you actually do your business how are you going to make money? Primarily there's going to be two ways, there's going to be selling your time and selling you essentially, and then there's going to be creating a product or a service that people can buy.

When you sell yourself, it's not a very scalable business

to get to earn more money. You're either going to have to raise your rates or you're going to have to hire more people like you and a lot of businesses do this. It's a great way to make a living and the beauty of this as well is there's essentially no cost, all you need is your laptop for a lot of these jobs and then a couple of pieces and then you go from there. Consulting is another way but it's very challenging to go beyond that if you want to sell a product or service. Find something that you're really passionate about living that lifestyle and taking that to the world, some people have found a lot of success by being on major E-commerce platforms.

Such people start off small and test to see what they want rather than marketing and building this giant plan with everything built out and all the things lined up. One can find success by simply doing it. That's one of the best advices that entrepreneurs can get, just do it, nothing is going to be perfect and perfection is the enemy of progress. A lot of the things that that you learn with businesses, you don't know what the market wants until you actually do it. Start small with a few products on your store and gradually add to this. Gradually you get wiser and smarter and then you can make your website an improve your marketing strategy.

If you don't know how to self-motivate and get yourself up fired up like this, then business isn't for you. In a world of business you're alone, there's not going to be somebody telling you every single thing. There's going to be people on the complete opposite side saying how horrible you are, constantly finding your legs. Think about it this way, any athlete that first gets into the league is picked on by everybody, they think he doesn't know how to play defence. As an an entrepreneur you've got to learn to keep yourself motivated and get your people motivated, you've got to learn how to self-motivate before you become an entrepreneur.

Save your money. How often do you save? The money you set aside will help you in the long term. Some of you might want to be in sales but don't know what to sell. This is perfectly ok you'll figure it out with time and research. You'll find out a way to make more money. Learn how to sell, your business not going to work if you don't know how to sell, you've got to learn how to sell so as an entrepreneur if you're an employee right now, you're working as if you didn't learn how to sell, what do you think happens? If you don't know how to sell, you've got to learn how to sell so before you make that plunge of becoming an entrepreneur full time learn how to.

Challenges of Being an Entrepreneur

Every entrepreneur will face challenges when building their company and future. One of these challenges is having self-doubt. we wanted to start with this one for a special reason, most businesses fail because people don't start then they fail by not taking the first step and this is because of self-doubt, you don't think you can achieve more but if history has taught us anything, it's that people are able to overcome their condition and grow. You don't have to see the end of the road to get in your car and start driving as long as you know where you're headed. You can go through life 1one step at a time.

Lack of resources it's easy to look at established players and see how much equipment resources and staff they have at their disposal rest assured they didn't start with everything like it is do not compare your level of success. In the beginning, you may lack resources, but you have time, a lot of it as well as, the enthusiasm to test, learn, and experiment your lack of resources forces you to be creative. That's your competitive advantage, you're not as rigid as everyone else. Sacrificing security once you get started on this road, you'll notice pretty quickly that it's not all rainbows and sunshine. Almost everything you make will go back into the business, you're working more hours than ever before and the future is still kind of uncertain.

Doubt starts kicking in and you don't know if you're going to make it safely. Lack of real support from those around you everybody around will encourage you to pursue your dreams because that's the nice thing to say to someone who's just starting a business but they are all monitoring your evolution and waiting for you to crash. Your family is blinded by their love for you and their support is irrational. Your friends care about your feelings but they have their own journeys to figure out. You're in this by yourself when she heads the fan you're the one who's going to have to clean it up and figure out how to move forward. Everyone wants to be there when you celebrate but all they're going to show is sympathy for your hardships and failures. If you want to support a friend who started a business, don't ask for a discount or a free service. Instead pay the full price and solve one of their problems.

Let's say you're looking to start an online store but have no idea where to start. You learn through trial and error but fortunately for you, the Internet is filled with tutorials and walkthrough helping you to navigate this terrain with ease. We're all a giant community of people holding each other’s hands as you try new things technical know-how may be intimidating at first but with time and practise you'll learn how to use the tools at your disposal. On top of that, it's never been easier or cheaper for that matter to start from scratch and build something the tools available right now are exponentially easier to use than ever before.

People start multimillion dollar businesses from their bedrooms and they do this by leveraging the tools billion dollar companies put at your disposal. If you're looking to start an online store, you can create one through the numerous website builders available. If you're looking for technical know-how, you need to start experimenting with these types of easy-to-use tools. Your ability to multitask can be challenging. New entrepreneurs don't expect this as you're under the impression that you'll be in your office overseeing everything that might become a reality later on down the road but in the early days you'll be doing everything, you're the sales agent, you're the manufacturer, you're the distributor, you're the support the manager and number one in charge of keeping it all together.

Many people just give up this happens because they lack the ability to create processes and delegate work. It might sound complicated but every business needs to do this if they hope to make it because being a one man or one woman show just isn't sustainable in the long run. Industry changes and your entire livelihood could be threatened by a change in the algorithm or by new laws and regulations this happens all the time in fast moving industries. A certain industry could be legalised or decriminalised only to be reversed in a few years once the people in charge of these decisions change. Other challenges faced includes taxes, lawyers, and more formalities. This is probably the most intimidating part of the journey, these people almost speak a different language from everyone else.

Rest assured that every entrepreneur goes through this, they are all confused in the beginning but as with everything we start to get a better understanding of the process as time goes by. Whenever faced with this type of bureaucratic issue look to the majority the same way you do with a drivers licence, almost everyone has one. You'll be fine in getting yours. Find, hire and fire employees. Employees can make or break a business, everyone thinks it's easy to find and keep good employees but everyone assumes that people want to work as hard as they do for the business only to be disappointed.

Finding the right people can be more difficult than you ever expect, these folks won't be able to read your mind, so you have to train them. They won't have the same drive as you and this will show in their performance, in time, you'll be forced to let some of them go. If you want to save your business, all of these will be major challenges you're going to have to overcome. Complete ownership of everything that happens is one of the greatest challenges that new entrepreneurs face. You need the mindset of taking ownership over what happens in your business because frankly you are the business you are responsible for everything if anything goes wrong it's because of a failure in your judgement or your failure in preparation

You train your employees, you set the values that targets the process. the brand you need to behave in accordance to everything the idea of taking complete ownership of everything that happens in your life is not new but most people stay away from it and live with the victim's mindset. Nothing is their fault, everything happens to them and they're just unlucky, those people actually fail in life because their success and happiness is entrusted to an external mystical force. What would happen if you flip that around and start acting like everything happens because you make it happen. You'll start seeing growth and a lot of it we became familiar with this after.

Another challenge most people don't realise is that they're going to have to deal with loneliness unless you find people who are dealing with the same type of struggles as you are. Most people won't be able to relate to your journey, they won't understand the level of stress you have to go through, the sleepless nights or the sheer amount of time that goes into building the life you want. Even if you go through all of this and in the event in which you do make it, it's still lonely at the top.

Almost everyone thinks that customers just happen, if you build it they will come. This might be true if you're building the only coffee shop in your city or have an unfair advantage in your demographic but for everyone else, you'll have to draw them in learn to market, tell stories, showcase your products and the benefits they offer your clients. You'll need to learn the skill of selling of differentiation and how to find new customer problems. Most people think of entrepreneurs as risk takers as people who risk it all with a dream of finding success in reality we're doing the exact opposite your job as an entrepreneur is to minimise risk what others may see as risky for you should be a game plan with a decent probability of success which is directly influenced by your aptitude and skills. You minimise risk by solving problems, other people don't know how to solve or find too difficult.

Competition is another challenge. Everyone wants your

attention and your money; you're no longer competing for customers with the business on the other side of the road now you're competing with everyone. The Internet has made it possible for people to sell their products all around the world so now customers have lots of options. You're going to have to stand out from the crowd and go head-to-head with everyone else who wants the same thing as you do. Lastly, an unavoidable challenge is failure so be ready to fail because you will. You'll have to face failures as an entrepreneur. You will try, you will plan, you're going to give it your all and you're still going to fail. It's likely that you aren't enough, you don't know enough, or you don't have enough. The challenge is to learn, adapt, and to try again that's how the world separates the real from the pretenders.

Starting a Business on a Low Budget

It is possible to start a business on a budget for even less than $500. There's really six things you can do to exchange what you're providing to the consumer with a customer for money and profits to you:

1. Providing a service for your customers
2. Giving advice because you're an expert your expertise is what the customer is paying for
3. Produce your model for 5 bucks you sell it for 20
4. Educate your customers
5. #5 you're giving me an experienced
6. Entertain your customers

All these six things, you and I spend money on every single day. All these six things are things you can figure out a way to start making money for yourself so now let's start off with services. Mobile auto detailing, this is the easiest thing to start off with, go get some equipment for less than $500 and to start servicing cars in your community. Another one is landscaping or running errands. You've got to use the skills that you have, for example, if you've got a brilliant voice how about you look into doing voice overs. You will find numerous freelance platforms online in which people will be willing to pay you 40 bucks just to do your voice for them. If you can put on different accents such as a British accent, it's an added bonus have a different type of an accent. You got voice overs for commercials to do, maybe you know how to do editing, writing editing, video editing, put yourself on a freelance platform. Maybe you know how to design websites and you know how to produce some for yourself, again go and sign up on a freelance platform and put yourself out. You have the talent, so provide your services for other people. Now, if you're reading this right now, you might be saying, "I want to start my own business, but I need a website" go on a freelance site and have somebody build a website for you. If it's hundred dollars try and look for a discount code to apply to the service.

If you're good at coaching, you might want to consider coaching kids on a specific type of sport. When people start off coaching kids, they can be getting around $50 for a 30-minute session. You might be surprised at how much they get paid, they're throwing a ball, they're doing all this other stuff because somebody else doesn't have the time to do it, but there's money in it. There are other businesses that you can do such as offering a massage service, you can give massages to multiple people in a session, let's say 20 people get massages at $50 each, that means that your business would get $1000 in that hour which is a decent amount of money to be made. You can make good sum of money if you're an expert at giving massages.

You can also start a notary license business, people need to motorize stuff and get fingerprint signatures, look into this because it's a lucrative business. Get the necessary qualifications you need to attain to be successful in this business and give it your all. You can really become an expert in investments if you put in the time and get clued up on the knowledge that you need. You can be an expert in insurance, you name it and you can get paid by insurance companies for offering your services. If you're more active and stronger physically and you know how to fight then you might want to become a security guard.

There are many ways that you can offer your services and start any good income on them. You don't always have to break the bank to have a lucrative career, just find out what you're good at and focus on that. If you look at you today, you'll see plenty of people using their talents to make money. You could be a brilliant graphic designer and use this skill to design book covers or magazines and make it a decent amount of money. Whatever you're doing just make sure that you enjoy it too, as you don't want to be miserable doing your job

Mistakes That Entrepreneurs Make

Someone can be an entrepreneur but not every entrepreneur has a successful business, screwing up from time to time is part of the entrepreneurial process. You often make mistakes and overnight success stories are often exaggerated and untrue, that is why you need to know about mistakes that new entrepreneurs make. One mistake that people make is that they treat their new business like a magical money vending machine, seriously it is the most common mistake made by all the new entrepreneurs. Most people who say that they want to start a new business are not actually looking for that at all, instead they just want a magical money vending machine where if they put $100 then they'll get $200 back but funnily enough it doesn't quite work that way here.

It doesn't work that way, most businesses take at least six months to turn a profit. Most of you would be thinking that's too long and they can get some profit as soon as they invest but that's extremely unlikely to happen because you see a business isn't some ambiguous thing you do to make money. For successful businesses you find or create great products, or services to sell and you can put those products in front of the right people. Give people a reason to buy your services. There is a learning curve at getting good at these things, some people are a genius at doing them naturally but like most things in life the majority of us will have to learn through education and experience.

Now, if you choose to live in a fairy tale land where you have unrealistic expectations of overnight success, then you can expect a failure rate of 99.9%. Another mistake that entrepreneurs make is that they are not spending enough money or spending too much money as a new entrepreneur. Money is likely to be one of your biggest concerns, pre-launch cash flow is likely to be close to nil, so making and saving money will usually take priority over everything else. There are two mindsets commonly seen among new entrepreneurs, either you have to spend money to make money or you will spend the bare minimum until you have some decent cash flow. All of these attitudes when taken to the extreme can be harmful, spend time building up your star-tup cash wisely but don't be afraid to invest in good people and quality products. This will bode well for you in the long term.

A common mistake that rising entrepreneurs make is that they either take too much advice from their expert people or they take none at all, intelligent input can make or break your business. Ignoring it or not soliciting it means you're flying blind, and your odds of success are low, on the other hand too much feedback has its own dangers. Develop relationships with a few experienced entrepreneurs who have both built and sold businesses within your industry. As a rule of thumb, choose advisers for specific parts of your business not the overall business mistake. Another failure to of the new entrepreneurs who want to do business is that when they start the business, they do not focus on the growth of their career.

Many new entrepreneurs are energetic and enthusiastic people but they can also be overly optimistic and pursue too many targets and directions at once. This typically results in mediocre results and this is why you should define your business mission. It's narrowly impossible when you move in too many directions at once especially in the early days of your business, you are likely to fail to execute anything directly so you end up working on the business instead of in the business. Another mistake made is that new entrepreneurs fail to follow up with clients, this is an important mistake that is made. Many new entrepreneurs are so often desperate to continually find new clients that they neglect the clients they already have and end up losing clients. Business statistics show that it takes seven more interactions to secure a new client or continue with a repeated client.

Develop and maintain a useful and organised follow up system to offer new services to your clients and don't let them slip away. Focus on being as authentic honest and truthful as possible in your way of selling. Sometimes new entrepreneurs try to do everything by themselves without taking anyone's help which is not a good thing, a big mistake that entrepreneurs make is thinking that they are all alone and they try to operate independently without surrounding themselves with wise counsel. Don't try to run a new business by yourself, find an onboard trustworthy seasoned advisers to discuss your business ideas, strategy challenges and progress.

As an entrepreneur, ideas will come and go if you need to get used to them going more than common not every idea is a good one and we tend to get carried away with the bad or impractical ideas than merely serve us in the long run. As a businessperson you need to listen to those around you and present yourself as a receptive person to receive honest and productive feedback. Becoming overly attached to your ideas can be dangerous and lead you holding on to and end implementing a bad idea. Learn to let go of ideas even those you are super passionate about. Another common mistake is that new entrepreneurs overthink taxes, not everybody likes taxes and one of the biggest benefits as an employee is that you don't even have to think about them, your employer automatically deducts it straight out of your paycheque.

While your employer takes care of your taxes, they still have a firm grip over your time and your time is what's most valuable but with business you can buy your time back and have enough money to hire an accountant to handle your taxes. In reality, you shouldn't fear starting a business because of taxes you don't have to deal with them with the money you make. You can easily hire an accountant to handle that area for you. Another mistake is that some new entrepreneurs don't know pivot through their early validation efforts. You're likely to gain feedback that you didn't anticipate, rather than throwing in the towel or ignoring what you've learned altogether, this should inspire you to change your business model to prevent failure. Many successful business ventures have come from calculating a new route, for example, Instagram began as a location based social network, uploading and sharing photos was just a feature, it was the feature users latched onto most so it was reborn as Instagram and well you know the rest of the story. This is also an essential point which mostly new people while doing businesses do. New entrepreneurs are sometimes afraid to invest and lose money. Sometimes people while doing business entrepreneurs are afraid to invest and lose their money and they are frightened of getting scammed.

Seeing instant returns on your money is never a realistic expectation, it's quite optimistic to think that your first add or product you are selling is going to be a home run win for your business but more often than not people have these expectations. They think that first product is going to be a winner for them or that their first landing page is going to convert into a big money. They start losing their confidence and they're afraid to invest more money in this field, but such a mindset is the only reason why a lot of people don't succeed. They want to hold tight to minimal risks yet have reap great rewards but that very mindset is what holds people back from achieving their success.

They aren't willing to invest money, they aren't willing to invest money. Those who end up successful are almost always ready to invest money because as mentioned before time is a valuable and appreciating asset. Get your time back. Part of achieving comes with the willingness to spend money on testing ads once you've spent the money to find a winning product, you can earn all that money back because you are willing to invest money into finding a winner but if you're fearful of losing money you'd never be able to find this out and you'll still find yourself stuck trying to move your business forward.

The Secret of a Successful Business

Now to answer the simple question everybody asks, if you're an entrapreneur your success can be guaranteed if you can answer this simple question, "How do I become successful?". You want to build a business that grows fast and makes a lot of money. Think about this, why do you buy some other brands that could do similar things that other brands can do? Your iPhone goes for half of the money people spend $100,000 on Rolex watches, when we can buy any watch that gives them time for $100. Why do we choose a brand and not others? Most of us would think that decision was based on some rational thinking well that's how consumers think. Several studies have proved that consumers choose brands based on any rational analysis, we make most of life's decisions based on emotions and that includes products and companies we've patronised. Now, if you agree with me, that man who buys no Rolex watch for $250,000 doesn't buy each thousand to cheque time. The woman who buys 1001 nights down in purse for $3.8 million doesn't buy that purse to carry her pick up sticks, the poor guy who borrows money to buy an iPhone and even the poor women who patronised Walmart all do it for a reason and that reason is arrived at after consumers ask the question "Why should you buy from you?" This is the simple question you must answer if you want to build a business that is fast and makes tonnes of money.

Humans are tribes. You really want to explain this concept very deeply so that you get it because when you understand this simple concept, it will change your business life forever. Some of us like to impress people so people might buy the Ferrari without cash, it doesn't matter whether you are in Asia or Europe, differences exist some of us love cheap things and would look for components for everything. Some of us love things to be fast everywhere, some of us don't mind if things are slow. Experts will handsomely pay for great services, some love quacks and they're also everywhere.

Think about why people post photos of their cars and watches on social media. Why do people post expensive phones? Why do we buy things we don't even need? It doesn't matter as long as people buy them. As an entrepreneur you must answer this question "Why should you buy from me?" This brings us to an important step in the process of building a green business and that's the concept of different season, business is not about competition and true businesses don't compete because competition kills. When Apple first released iPhone in June

2007 Steve Ballmer made joke about The Alchemist remove selling $400 sleep laughed and called bold a joke. Today, Apple sells phones for prices as high as $1500 and people line up to buy these. One reason is because apple isn't competing.

Success doesn't happen overnight, but if you keep on align in your mindset towards your dreams you will eventually achieve what you want. Make yourself your greatest competition and power forward with your plan, business is about being innovative, creative and motivated. Don't give up at your first hurdle that you come across but take it as a lesson to be successful in the future.

Patience is the Key to Success

Think about the most discouraging event that took place in your life, it could be you were expecting to marry a girl or guy, everything was going well until you get that text message saying "I don't think this is going to work" and that's it they break up with you and that's when life gets confusing. It's like working for boss of yours and he tells you if you do XYZ and you hit these numbers you are going to get a promotion. You had all those numbers it comes down for promotion time and he gives a promotion to someone else, not to you. You're discouraged, maybe you've got great ideas but no one's listening to you, maybe you're sitting and financially you're in the same exact situation for 2-3 years. What do you need to do? The most discouraging times were when you're putting effort and you're not seeing progress or results this can psychologically mess with you to not believe that enough effort is going to produce progress and for the rest of your life, you're just going to be like "Well, even if I give my best nothing's going to happen."

Even if you love this person, nothing's going to happen even if you give them your best year savings, nothing's going to happen. You need to understand and manage expectations and there's a certain level of patience you need to have. You can create timelines for yourself. Here's an example of what a good timeline looks like in order to see any glimpses of positive change. One can take about 21 days and the second one is 90 days, anything you do to your business matters. A new idea can be implemented, you can say to yourself, "Here's what we're going to start do every weekend?" The first week you might get no results, the second week no results, the third week no results, the 4th now results are showing, the 5th week a little more result and so on until the 90 days are up and things have taken shape.

If you want to make a real massive change, it will probably take take 10 to 20 years, but you would get the kind of results that you're dreaming of. You may be the only person in your family that James big and maybe everybody thinks your idea we never materialised, but as a potential entrepreneur you have to keep your dream alive through motivation and perseverance and not losing sight of the goal.

There are two qualities that can increase your chances of success one of them is patience and the second one is persistence. Patience is learning to handle the passing of time, now once you've had an appetite for success and you start going for it, now you've got to learn to handle the passing of time. It takes time. It takes time to build a corporate work of art, it takes time to build a Symphony Orchestra with flawless music and harmony that sends you on flights of ecstasy to be remembered long after the orchestra has shutdown and the lights have gone out. It takes time to put harmony together, it takes time to build a life, it takes time to build a successful business that you can be proud of. It takes time to get through school it takes time to develop and grow.

Give your goals time, give your business time If you're in management, give your people time. If you're a parent give your kids time don't be too quick give them time now not forever but the time, it takes time. Here's the ultimate challenge, you've got to have patience with yourself it takes time to make changes in habit and discipline it takes time to correct all errors in judgement and to finally give up old blame and pick up new responsibility. It's takes you time to succeed in what you want, some people blame the government or blame taxes, the company, or blame the marketplace and rarely blame themselves. This blame game may take a long time for such people to give up.

Be patient with yourself is the first step and while you're dealing with the passing of time. Number two is to keep doing it, be persistent, be tenacious, keep doing it. As long as you are patient and persistent, it's hard to elude success as long as you maintain patience, persistence and tenacity. There's only one person, just one person that will draw the line between success and failure one person and that person is you so be patient, be persistent, you need both patience and persistence together and here's why lack of patience is probably the worst enemy of ambition.

While your ambition keeps growing, keeps moving, keeps looking for new ways to succeed impatience tends to grow frustrated impatience won't allow for persistence. Impatience wants to give up, impatience calls discouragement failure but your ambition won't let you give up so easily, not if you're persistent. What others may call failure, ambition calls a learning opportunity, a chance to make adjustments along the charted course to success. Ambition knows something else too, ambition knows that the longer the achievement is incoming, the more valued it is. You can look at a few aspects of patience, some examples that might help illustrate just how valuable it is. There are six aspects of patients and number one is knowing when an opportunity is right and when more preparation is needed. Let's say you're opening up a restaurant specialising in fresh seafood, you're all excited to get going get the money coming in instead of it all going out. You're all excited so because you're all excited you want to open early during patients gets the best of you and so you do open before your scheduled grand opening.

Customers start coming in, they're all excited about this new great restaurant and everybody wants some fresh seafood. They're all ordering fresh seafood from the menu but now you panic, you haven't got anything, you're not ready, the fresh seafood shipment won't come in for a week, impatience has just killed the restaurant. Now, let's say you've got a great new product that's scheduled to come out on the market in the next several months. Everything is going according to plan, so you start planning your ads and start planning big public relations events. You're so sure that it's going to happen that you set a date the engineer told you that the product is not ready but you're sure it will be. You started planning everything and invite lots of people influential people that are buyers of your product.

You're so excited that you went ahead without the product actually being done come. The week of the grand unveiling the engineers come to you and say it still doesn't work, your impaticncc just lost you credibility in the marketplace. Patience is important and knowing the difference between when the opportunity is right and when more work needs to be done. Remain alert even if opportunity doesn't come right away, make sure that your patience allows you to keep your eyes open and ready for opportunity. Keep looking and be patient. Prepare for opportunities, even if there's a delay, even if things aren't going just the way you think they should. Keep your disappointments at Bay and keep getting ready for opportunities. Be prepared, always be prepared and don't let impatience allow you to give up on good opportunities.

Take the little setbacks in stride, take the little successes in your stride, don't let small disappointments discourage you, don't let the little successes dilute you. Avoid the emotional rollercoaster that will always disrupt your plan. If you're waiting on the decisions of others, be patient, you cannot control the decision-making abilities of others, you cannot control their timing. If your project was to come up before the board in one meeting and time ran out, and they moved your project to the top of the agenda for the next meeting be patient, don't be frustrated about what you have no control over. Take a vacation from your ambition if you've been working day after day, week after week, month after month, without a break, take a vacation from your ambition. The patient person secure in their ambition knows that the drive and ambition will still be there even after some time off as a matter of fact with some time off the ambition will have a stronger pull than ever.

When you come back through, persistence is patience inaction, persistence is always looking for new opportunities, persistence is courageous, it doesn't give in to fear. Persistence is hopeful, it doesn't let discouragement through the door, persistence is positive, it keeps you on track with your plans and your goals and the last thing is that persistence is cheerful, not gloomy. Cheerful persistence knows the gloom and depression and disappointments waste energy, cheerful is created patience and persistence are both required for success. Success is something you had tracked by the person you become, success is not something you pursue what you pursue usually eludes you, like a butterfly something you go after that you can't catch. Success is something you attract like a magnet by the person you become.

To attract attractive people you must be attractive, to attract powerful people you must be powerful, to attract committed people you must be committed. Instead of going to work on them you go to work on yourself, you work harder on yourself than you work on the job and if you become you can attract. The whole key is to make yourself valuable, the key is to make yourself attractive, the key is to make yourself skilful, competent, willing, powerful, unique, and sophisticated. The whole key really to the future is personal development because the greatest gift you can give to someone else is your personal development self-development and self-investment. If you become 10 times wiser, 10 times stronger, 10 times brighter, 10 times more competent, think of what that will do for your success.

If you grow, think of what that will do for your future. self-development firms success, self-investment earns respect and the only way to make a better investment in your future is to become better and stronger and wiser and more competent and the more effective you become the more attractive you are and the more attractive you are the more you attract success. Self-development and self-investment attract success, that's powerful! Now here's what would be pitiful, if your income grew and you didn't grow because here's what usually happens if your income takes some jumps, it's best that you grow quickly up to where your income is why because otherwise your income will soon come back to where you are. Success doesn't want to hang around an incompetent person. That's the problem with winning the lottery, the lack of self-development to be able to master it and keep it and now the fortune is bigger than the person rather than the person being bigger than the fortune. If you're a parent, use that as a challenge to grow personally use the challenge of parenting to grow see what you can become.

Why Entrepreneurs Fails?

There are many reasons why entrepreneurs fail but in this section 10 main reasons will be listed. Take notes and tried to avoid making these mistakes if you want to be successful in your entrepreneurial journey.

1. Lack of Skills:

You need the skills to pay the bills, if you don't know how to sell and market and negotiate and lead people and do things that your business requires, then you won't be an asset. You need skills to help you to move higher in your entrepreneurial journey. Such skills can be acquired through practise or learning, it can also be acquired through experience in running your business. You might notice that there's a specific skill or expertise that you really need to have, learn it yourself, there's no way you can ever to that desired position until you get equipped with the necessary skills or knowledge. Ask yourself, "What are the top three skills that you need to acquire in the next 12 months?" and work steadily on achieving those skills.

2. Lacking in Other areas:

you may have a lack of drive, motivation or energy that is required to take your business to the next level. A lot of people think that a business is just a job that they just clock in and clock out for 40 hours a week for the next 40 years. However, that's not how it is, you have to dedicate all your time and energy as well as will power to make that business succeed. There are experiences that might knock you down, but you have to be strong and get back up. The marketplace will tell you exactly what to do and if you have to drive that energy, willpower and motivation to take constructive criticism and apply in your life. Lack of motivation ends up killing most entrepreneurs when there's a setback or an adversity some entrepreneurs actually say, "I can't take anymore, it's too hard, you quit," but that's not you, you're not going to stop, you're going to keep on going because you know exactly what it takes to get to the next level.

3. Poor planning:

some businesses haven't been planned well at all, they think they can just jump into the business and somehow it'll work and some way along the way they're going to learn but the fact is that that's not how it works. There are so many people that have been taught that they have to fail their way to success and they end up jumping into business planning to fail. This is not success. What you need to focus on are the things you need to learn, the things you need to do, and the tactics and techniques you need to apply to make your business prosper.

4. Starting business for the wrong reasons

Some people get into business with the sole intention of making a lot of money or just to prove certain people wrong, but you need to understand exactly what you want out of your business for it to succeed. It's OK to want money, it's OK to want to accomplish something and feel good about that accomplishment but if you don't have a solid plan in place, it's never going to work. Think about how you can add value to the marketplace, if you have the right idea, the right plan and the right reasons, then your business will succeed.

5. Neglecting the business

So many people who have started businesses think that you and take you out. The marketplace does not play, it doesn't joke because they're making a lot of money, they can just sit back have a Margarita at the beach and relax with your friends. This will kill your business because if you know that there are things to do and you're not doing them, eventually they're going to catch up with you, it's only a matter of time. If there's things you have to change and you ignore these things, eventually everything will go downhill.

There are so many businesses that neglect essential details and it ends in up having costly consequences. Imagine driving along the highway at night-time and seeing a sign that's missing a couple letters blacked out because they haven't changed the lights and now people can't recognise that business because they can't read the sign. Maybe they know what the business is, but they realise that those people don't care about that business. Ask yourself "What are somethings that are easy to do that you haven't done already?" If you've been neglecting important areas and tasks of your business, it's time to change!

6.Choosing a poor location for your business

If you have an online business, you might think it doesn't matter where you're located but if you're trying to do business with people in a different country and you represent a country that they're not familiar with, that can turn them off. "What is being implied here?" Let's say you're from an obscure country and you're reaching out to people that live in America for people that live in England or people that live in Australia or any well-developed country, most likely you have a good idea of what product or service you want to offer.

Let's say you understand exactly what kind of client you want but if you look at their perspective, you've got to fully comprehend that they may not understand where you're coming from. They don't know what you're about, they don't understand the culture so this might create some barriers between them and your business.

7. Expanding your business too soon

maybe you have an idea and want to get to a different location to make it happen faster. You might set high goals for yourself to achieve and take risks but then you fail because you tried to do it too soon. Maybe you haven't done it at all, maybe you have a business that needs to expand but you're too afraid to get into that next location, you're too afraid to take the risk and so you end up suffering and losing capital because of your decision.

You have to know exactly what to expect. there might be times in your business where you're flooded with work but you know you need to expand. What you need to do is plan for the next six months with the next year and try to figure out a way that you can make that leap and expand your business. You have to take control of your business and not let your business take control of you, the best thing you could do is surround yourself with resource so people that can make things easier for you once you make that decision to expand, you'll be able to take all your resources leveraged into your advantage and finally that expansion follows.

8. Lack of capital

Now, this might sound obvious and a lot of people probably face this before but there's always something you can do about it. You could always make sales and make sure your product and services actually get out there. You can take a loan; you could use credit cards or you can take investments. There's always a way for you to gain capital and if you have to come up with those ideas, you might have to sell your car, you might have to even sell your house or take out a second mortgage or run your credit card. No matter what your situation is you've got to find a way to stay afloat and keep your business running.

You've got to find the capital to keep it going. Many of us have faced unpleasant situations before, empty bank balances, maxed out credit cards, overdrafts, and other financial difficulties but if you're tough enough and you understand exactly what to do with your money, you will find that capital and you will make it happen. If you want to run a business, you can't run a business without learning how to deal with people. Always there and business is all about people you always have to put people first there's some entrepreneurs that put their business first and if you get about people and eventually people will realise that. Understand the leadership style that you have, understand the leadership skills that you need to gain understanding about exactly what you need to do. You become a more effective leader so you can make your business grow to where you wanted to be.

9. Lack of honesty

The lack of integrity, the lack of character, entrepreneurs really want to make it big they really want to succeed in their business but if you're not telling the truth, the marketplace will sniff you out. People will realise if you're lying to them. If you're cheating them you'll realise if your prices aren't the same with the other people that you serve and if you're not telling the truth. If you're not honest with the people you're dealing with then eventually you'll be found out. Abraham Lincoln once said that you can fool some of the people somc of thc timc, but you cannot fool all of the people all the time.

To make sure you're honest with yourself, the people you deal with and eventually the marketplace will reward you for your honesty. These are the main reasons why entrepreneurs fail and if you're on train or are you thinking about becoming one, make sure to incorporate as many of these points as possible.